Each Stitch to Build a Heart

Mackenzie Angeconeb

Copyright © 2025 by Mackenzie Angeconeb

All rights reserved. No part of this publication may be reproduced or transmitted in any form or by any means, electronic or mechanical, including photocopying, recording or any information storage and retrieval, without the written permission of the publisher. Names, characters, places and incidents are either the product of the author's imagination or used fictitiously, and any resemblance to actual persons living or dead, events or locales is entirely coincidental. All trademarks are properties of their respective owners.

Published by
BookLand Press Inc.
15 Allstate Parkway, Suite 600
Markham, Ontario L3R 5B4
www.booklandpress.com

Printed in Canada

Front cover design by Wendy Beaulieu

Library and Archives Canada Cataloguing in Publication

Title: Each stitch to build a heart / Mackenzie Angeconeb.
Names: Angeconeb, Mackenzie, author.
Series: Modern Indigenous voices.
Description: Series statement: Modern Indigenous voices
Identifiers: Canadiana (print) 20250243334 | Canadiana (ebook) 20250244373 | ISBN 9781772312577 (softcover) | ISBN 9781772312584 (EPUB)
Subjects: LCGFT: Poetry.
Classification: LCC PS8601.N45786 E13 2025 | DDC C811/.6—dc23

We acknowledge the support of the Government of Canada through the Canada Book Fund. We acknowledge the support of the Canada Council for the Arts. We acknowledge funding support from the Ontario Arts Council and the Government of Ontario.

Each Stitch to Build a Heart

To my husband,
the strongest stitch in my heart.

I

the friends we gather and lose
in the crucial times of development
lay the foundation
for who we will become
and who we will seek out
as we continue to grow into life

did you know that i had to be shown how to skate twice?
the flat edge blades that i was comfortable with
did not have my size
i sat alone on the bench, watching others fly by with ease
my cheeks flushed with embarrassment
under the chilled air

before this, i did try and fell on my first step out
holding the boards or a chair while my feet
did not cooperate atop the ice
hearing the childish taunts made my vision blurred
and i gave up

you skated in front of me, showing me visually
how to move on curved blades
encouraging me to try one more time
i declined, afraid of the ridicule that would follow
if i tried again

you offered me your gloved hand,
saying you would keep me safe

always someone to spend
the empty nights
left alone with

never too far
and always ready
to walk

we lasted many years
going from acquaintances
to best friends
to wannabe-partners
and back to acquaintances

out of all my friendships,
i thought ours would succeed
against the passing of time

sometimes i walk too fast
and have to stop for others to catch up

it never fails to remind me
of when i struggled to keep up with you

we orbited around
one another
for years

always read to walk
or run turkey trails
or ditch class

never venturing deep
to the troubles
we both felt

my first trip was with you
grandkids driven across borders to the casino
how we stayed occupied has faded
but this, i remember:
shopping in the stores not in our country
buying my favourite shirt that has since found a new home
the surprising bitter taste of sweet tea
throwing away the treasured pencil sharpener
i brought with me

we pretended we were sisters
and tried to swap the ones we did have

living at each other's houses on the weekends
our hair always smelt of salt water

and we always got the treats
that i still love to this day

we lived at the pool
playing mermaids
and seeing who could hold their breath the longest

it was there in the room
with steamy windows and freezing water
that i first spoke of a secret
i did not yet understand

and by the time i did understand
we had begun to drift apart

as i walk through the sandpit
in search of raspberries atop a wasp's nest
i am reminded of when the sand became mud

the cracking feeling of it dried to our skin
the dusty smell in my nostrils
the sucking sound it made as we rolled and crawled

we often played dirty
and often made each other cry
but in the end i will always see mud in place of sand

we shared the same identity
and yet
you never felt the crisis
that i continue to battle

we sat in your living room
as i marveled at the bookcases
and wished i could read as well as you

now i can
and i am so excited to read
the novel you will one day write

we were not as close as some
but we were fiercely supportive
of one another

and i think
that is all you need
in a friend

after you moved
we did not stay in contact

but we did message each other twice
both times for condolences

i have never told you
that when i lay asemaa down for him
i lay some down for them as well

the trees we played around are being thinned out
and our enchanted forest is now a parking lot

the streams and chasms we played in
have been filled in with dirt

there is construction
where there once was long grass

so much has changed
and yet i think of you there

i remember that you
always felt so sure of yourself
in everything you did
and all i wanted
was to experience
what that is like

your house was huge
and perfect for slumber parties
we would double up on the two bunk beds
giggling all night

you were the hyperactive friend
that i always secretly envied
for reasons i still do not understand

you switched schools
and we all cried

later, i saw you in the halls
and wanted to say hi

but i never did
and i still don't know why

i would hear the ringing impact
and see the dust fall on your face
for years,
i would see a chipped tooth in my reflection
but i could also feel the uncontrollable laughter
that was responsible

the slightest drop of sugar
and you were bobbing around
on the bouncing chair

words jumbling over themselves
an ecstatic expression
spread into a grin

you never bothered to hide
the buzzing in your body
empowered in your hyperactivity

the two of us and a puppy
sharing an apple on a sunny day
sitting on the aging porch

i can't remember why i was there
whether it was a sleepover or a visit
but i remember the peace of that afternoon

you were the first person i told
when i tried to accept that i like women

it was met with an inappropriate response
and i never told another person for several years

once again,
you were the first person i told a secret to

it was met with a childish response
followed by attempts to take back
all the times you were cruel

it felt like a teeter-totter
feeling great and filled with giggles
or being forced to laugh along,
while i hurt inside

getting off the teeter-totter
was one of the best choices
i ever made

i never felt bad about my appearance
and connection to the culture
until you

fifteen years later,
and i still spend every summer contemplating
using cooking oil instead of sunscreen

on the surface
it seemed as if
all was well
and how dare
anyone assume
differently

i read aloud
that bananas helped sad people
and you offered to bring me one for lunch
every day

i waited for your boisterous laugh to explode out
but it did not come
i was touched by your sincerity
and gladly ate the few you brought me

the grassy field we used to play in
is a construction site now

the pine trees in the yard
that we pretended were forests
have been cut down

the house i lived in changed from pink to blue
the house you live in changed from white to grey

what i am saying is
the physical may have changed
but our memories remain

your parents knew of my home
before i understood
and made sure to let me know
that i was always welcome

we were neighbours
even when you moved
and were inseparable
until i moved

a log cabin on a river peak
drafty but warmed by a wood stove
falling asleep listening to your blaring headphones

searching for four leaf clovers
practicing our cart wheels
and judging your screamo singing

your mother's voice on the boat warning
that it was too choppy to drive fast
hiding the tiny dog in our sweaters
against the eagles up high

your laughter rings clear
through my memories
as if it is happening
in present time
and i find myself wishing
that i was as bold as you

playing card games in the sky dome
and burning our hands with the communal sink

watching the skies
and wishing on shooting stars

watching the sunrise
and keeping an eye out for that hidden rock

before sleepovers fell away to parties,
i had my first breakup and couldn't sleep

as the sun began to rise,
i took your moms keys

daisies in locks
and foggy fields
and whining pop punk

i came back when the sun was warming the air
feeling renewed and at peace,
i crawled back into your cozy bed

as with many others,
we simply faded out of each others lives

but i will always cherish our time together
and see you as one of my closest friends

we mixed blue dye into the bread machine
and sprinkled cinnamon sugar on the jam

comparing our egg scrambling techniques
and debating on fluffy or crumbled

we drank rooibos tea
and worshipped impractical egg-shaped lipbalm

the past was left alone
the future was yet to come

the present was what
really mattered to you

it was a wonderful opportunity

we had a bonfire on a frozen beach
i went bowling for the first time

and i got to see you every week

the first time i really saw you
we were in the basement of a church

it was the first time i accepted
i could have feelings for a girl

your family belonged to that church
and i continued to crush from afar

i wonder how my life would've changed
had i known the church didn't mind you liking girls

we often shared friends
and even as my childhood crush faded
i saw you on occasion
but did not attempt to become friends
because of the boy i never truly believed

my feelings for you
changed over time

from silent crush
to silent competition

only another person
with our shared diagnosis category
would understand
the envy i feel

we learned that liquids could have different weights
not in science class
but in glass cups and hidden bottles

giggling and roughhousing as we always did
bugging your brothers as we always did

confused when i awoke
covered in wax
and you sleeping on the floor

your house became the hang out spot
across from the park that is no longer there

squishing six girls on a trundle bed
built for two

we were hardly alone
and it always felt like a home

you went back home once more
and just like that,

we were strangers
waving hi as we passed

that crack of lightning smile
with the accompanying jingling laugh
always comes to mind
when i am on the sidewalk
that lead to your house

proudly wearing
your brother's clothing
and painting your nails
in hot pink

never once
feeling as if
you had to choose
between the two

it is a precious thing
that only a select few friends
had devices

or there would be a video somewhere
with us smacking our heads on the wall
as we shot our bodies across the hall

sitting in a friend's garage, left open
sharing swiped smokes
watching the clouds and discussing the importance of bees

we were the ones left behind when everyone went home
not close in school
but filling up our days with each other that summer

the marvel of social media
is watching stories of an old friend
and seeing another old friend in it
smiling widely the same way she always did

laying back on a bed of clovers and honeysuckles,
watching the clouds roll and form shapes
i remember the day we walked all over town
trying to fill up our summer days
outside of babysitting and laying on the beach

i have met
very few people
who do not
pretend humans
are not animals
and you
are one of them

sitting on the weathered porch
sharing a king size

you: saying you weren't solid enough for them yet
me: sucking it to the filter

an easy afternoon with overcast skies
and a friendship i wish continued as we grew

you were north side
and i was south side

you remembered the two red heads
with the native girl walking by
i remembered the kids
stopping to watch us on the playground

casual friends in our final year
as the *big kids*

becoming the youngest again
simmered away the relationship we had

but we continue to say hi
and smile in passing

some days
for work or for martial arts

i walk the hallways
we often sat to do our assignments

i see the windowsills we shared our secrets on
and use the stairwells we cried in

you decided to become lefthanded
on a whim one day

i watched as you flexed
your newly aching hand

as you forced your body
to try something new

years later,
i handed you a pen

and saw that
you never gave up

we always made pancakes
on the lopsided coils

and asked for strawberry cream cheese
with strawberry eyes

to this day,
i do not remember how
we became best friends
for a summer

we were just convenient
for each other
i had my first job
and you knew who to contact

but it is as clear as crystal
in my mind
when i released my fear
and said yes

we despaired at the news
and decided to go wild one last time

but two days before
was my intended last day

that rusty boat is still there
and i cringe at the thought
of how often we sat
and tried to convince each other
it wasn't green

you knew exactly who you were
and were unapologetic about it
to the point that it felt
a bit excessive and bloated
but you were you
and refused to be anything else

to this day,
your laugh and your kind words
are held close
in my heart

a confidant
following our secret blogs

orbiting around each other
with the knowledge we did not share

you knew my brother better than you knew me
and yet i wish we had been closer

i see you around and i think to myself,
i hope things are finally working for you
rather than against you

while i hid
and dared not let
my pain see the sun
you embodied the ways
we tried to feel alive

what i now know is called body breaks
often meant we were shooting hoops
through the entry way
and trying not to hit the lights

or passing a soccer ball
in a circle
until it got too aggressive
and the vent came crashing down

i like to think
that i was the one person
you didn't feel like
you had to act tough around

four of us came to school
on the day the teachers made us leave

we decided to walk the tracks
and scale the rock face

later we returned
and sat on the bright stage

not thinking that
we would never see each other again

you were such a typical nish boy
that when i see

the track pants
and
hoodie
and flat brim hat

i often wonder
if it is you
all grown up

from the day i saw
the beaded brim hat
and heard the songs
emerge from your throat
i wanted so badly
to switch places with you

II

one day,
we are choosing our classes
promising to remain friends
despite the different streams
and the next,
we are surrounded
by new friends
and expectations
in a time
when our world feels
as if it may implode

sitting on your trampoline
laughing and jumping
the sun put highlights in your hair
and a part of me wanted your hand in mine

the first genuine friend
after years of bullies masked as friends,
meant more to me
than you could ever imagine

i impulsively cut my hair into bangs
when i should've been studying for the exam
we crammed in the hallway for
after,
we held each other
and sobbed uncontrollably

fallen leaves on dewy grass
both always arriving early
we would sit and enjoy the slowly crowding halls
on break,
we would sit outside
and allow ourselves to be kids
instead of playing at young adults

settling for what was comfortable
or what felt safe in that moment
was not an option for you

a few months before we could sign
for the piercings ourselves,
we took an afternoon trip to the next town
for the tattoo shop that always lopsided my piercings

speeding around a vehicle and
laughing as we pulled over immediately
to defog the windows

screaming in pain
as we stepped out of the shop
into the freezing winter air

walking on a glass floor
both aware of the other

so alike and yet so different
above all else we understood

our parallels
slowly began to drift
in our final year

as always,
you supported
my escape

and i will
support you from afar
as always

i still listen to
our favourite high school singer

and as i did back then,
i mistake her voice for yours

if i could use one word
to say how you seemed to me,
it would be: unafraid.

when i stopped sleeping
and would wander the roads
staring up at the vast array of stars

we began to meet
huddling in the hidden blanket
and watch the sunrise

i always was the Mom Friend
taking care of and nurturing others

with you by my side,
i got to experience it

the last time we hung out
i fell asleep on a dog bed
and woke up with the towel you covered me with

our last hurrah,
spent laughing at comedy specials
and sharing sprinkled icing

debating brands of cigarettes
opening up about the toxicity
holding each other's cold hands

i wonder who ended up
with our polaroids

the cloudy ones with a pressed faces
each of us with spray cans in hand
and coloured hair

you maintained a softness
to all that mattered to you
even on your worst days

seeing your smile spread
across a freckled face

as i reassured you
of your talent with a sponge
and low budget animation

always made
my days easier

trying to write a poem
about a friendship

with the one i spent
secretly loving

never ends up being
about a friendship

i had a plan:
to engrave 'prom?'
into a potato for you

but as with everything
involving you,
i was too afraid

you are everywhere

in the rivers
in the forests
in the sinking building
in the produce aisle

and everything in between

to see the stars
move across
the sky
as you smiled
was enough for me

you were the first person i told
as i tried not to cry in the empty halls
as you tried to remove

the person you knew
from the person i knew

you provided unwavering support
as i told my mistakes
as you assured me it was not my fault

how unfortunate it is
a verge of a deep friendship
being pushed aside
from the complexities of our lives

i had the picture of us three printed
intending to put it in a photo album

it sits in the hideaway of my coffee table
to one day be gazed upon again

as i remembered the gratitude i felt for you
and the tears i forced back as we said 'cheese'

anytime i am gifted
a foil wrapped egg

my words of warning
ring clear in my ears

the intensity boiled beneath
all of who you showed
yourself to be

occasionally bubbling up
and spilling over
to the surprise of others

we sped through the rivers
talking while we waited

it made perfect sense the path you choose
and you congratulated me on mine

what could have been a solid friendship
or perhaps in another life, more

was kept at an arms length
due to the pressure from others

the last time i saw you as a friend,
you were half buried in the sand
as i turned you into a mermaid

the next time after,
you were in coveralls
and i worked two buildings over

you were once
on the outskirts of my life

living next to the pink house
that later turned blue

and you have since
been added to my memories

as one of the only people
who tried everything to keep me safe
from myself

you held hope
for what must have been
a tiring stretch
and yet
you were happy
when it wasn't you

on a hot day nearing the end of school
when the portables would turn into ovens

we sat outside on the steps
discussing our shared favourite series

when you abruptly expressed sadness
at my way of keeping myself alive

never close as children
barely close as teenagers

the only ones who read the same books
the only ones from the community

you were still one of my closest friends
and i hope i was one of yours

you moved yet again,
but that was not the end for us

i moved on from the one you called tyler
to the person you saw as a brother

our paths have crossed occasionally since,
and will continue as time goes on

there are books on my shelf
that are not mine

freely given to borrow
and 'regretfully' not returned

if something seemed to be
out of your reach
you removed the obstacle

and accomplished
your goals until
a new one arose

III

life always felt
as if i needed to follow
a structure
as if it was
laid out for me
and i tried to create this
without much thought
to what i really wanted
and needed at the time

on a school trip
from slopes i was not good at

we sat together on the bus
and partially fell asleep

the whispers of our friends
and the clicks of their devices

my first experience at letting the thoughts of others
determine my actions

giving into what i thought
i should want

luckily it ended
before we got too far

we were playing at being older
not ready for what an 'us'
could really mean

we would text late at night
when i was at the point
i needed to close one eye to see straight

it has been so long
that i do not remember
what we talked about

but i do remember
the butterflies in my ribcage
and the warmth in my smile

sometimes
finding safety
when you
need it
the most
is all
that matters

cold feet and crunching leaves
my hand is missing in yours

the expression on your face
but no longer seeing your features

your burning hands
scorching my skin

a rock skipping over the water

the laughter,
the underage immaturity masking as cuteness,
the effort to be older than we were

hitting the water

the secrets,
the waiting for it to be over,
the feeling of dread mixed with hope

always ends with drowning

we ended as we began
at 7:32 pm on a tuesday

instead of a slow heaviness
settling into my body

this time,
i felt a release

you are everywhere
and in everything i do

for so long
all i wanted
was to be rid of you

or to have the love
i thought was true

i tried to create what i thought
was needed to be happy
to the point that i was forcing
what was long dead
to fight for breath
when all i needed
was to let go

i loved your smile
the genuine one

and when it came time
for you to say cheese

i did everything i could
to ensure that smile
was captured

i have always been afraid
it is my underlying emotion

and i have missed out
on a lot because of that

but the thing i regret the most
is never telling you how i truly felt

it was years
after we faded away

that i realized
and my heart clenched

that anyone on the outside
looking in

would forget about
the boy i called war

and see us
instead

every time i walk into the store
i see the foods
we always grabbed

on a hike
as i run along the roots
i feel your warmth

you are everywhere
and a part of me
will always wonder

too late
i realized
who i was

and i ached
for what
could have been

IV

when households got routers
instead of fighting between
making a call
and using the internet,
schools took to training us
on how to be safe in this new world
and warned against the very people
that would later become
my best friends

i left the arid drop-off turn
and followed the invisible thread
eyes searching
and finding your mother
with you trailing behind

the messages come and go
sometimes going on for hours
others taking several weeks
but we are always there
waiting for the other

on the eve of my birthday

we were looking for a buddy
to exchange stats and motivation
we were not expecting

to make a best friend

after a week of
long drives and blistered toes
constant takeout and checking menus
tarot cards and a box of donuts
we shared an imported bottle
and took the polaroid
that i use as a bookmark

you are worlds away
existing in a different time
than when we first met

we have both come so far
from being lonely teenagers
in the dark

each living a life
of our own
for the first time

the rhythm of spoken sound
rising and falling

the focus is not on the meaning
but the vibrations hitting the ears

hearing your laughter for the first time
became one of my favourite songs

we are a collection
of laughs from afar

we are so alike
that it is suspicious

we are the sisters
we always needed

first, a follow
and then casual interaction

second, a message or two
and then sharing other socials

third, phone numbers
and then calling whenever we wanted

i take him to the witch store for the first time
and point out pieces of your practice
while trying to find the items of mine

you are a shooting star
in a bleak sky
providing a flash of fire
with the promise of dancing lights

Acknowledgements

I would like to start by thanking everyone who I have written about in this poetry collection. They will remain nameless, but if they happen to read this, they will know which poems are about them. Thank you for being a part of my life. I wouldn't be who I am today without you.

A special thanks to my husband for his unwavering support of my writing, even when I do it while watching his karate classes. His stitch prompted me to write poetry about everyone who I have loved, romantic or not.

A huge thanks to the staff at Bookland Press. Without all your hard work, my poetry would not be in the hands of the world.

A final thank you goes to Evan J. We met once when I attended your workshop during the pandemic and you gave me the inspiration to pursue poetry again.

www.ingramcontent.com/pod-product-compliance
Lightning Source LLC
Chambersburg PA
CBHW061748070526
44585CB00025B/2833